The Turtle's Wish

Barbara Laban

Illustrated by **Meilo So**

OXFORD
UNIVERSITY PRESS

Letter from the Author

I stumbled upon my first Chinese characters when I was about seven years old. I saw them on the inside of a small paper umbrella. It took me a while to figure out that the umbrella was made out of old Chinese newspapers. Years later, still fascinated by this first encounter, I decided to study Chinese.

Some time ago, I left my home country of Germany and have since lived in Taiwan, the Netherlands and now the UK. However, long before setting foot abroad, I was already travelling the world between the pages of all the books I read. With that in mind, I'm excited that I can take you to Beijing to meet Paulina and Weiting.

Luckily everyone in my family shares my passion for books and listens patiently to my ideas. The only exception is Mia, the cat, who often tries to sabotage my work by sitting on my keyboard. Which is maybe why I chose to feature a pet turtle in this story ...

Barbara Laban

Chapter One

I can't write a single word.

Strange, you might think. Especially for a girl of 11 who has gone to school almost every day since she was four years old.

Of course, it is not entirely true. I can write in English, the language I speak with Mum and Dad at home, but after five years in Beijing – China's capital city – I still couldn't write a single Chinese character even if I wanted to.

Dad says it doesn't matter. Mum, on the other hand, is quite concerned. When we go to the shops I can translate for her, but as soon as I have to read or write, it's over. She always says she wishes I'd give it a try, but you don't need to learn Chinese when you go to my school. All our classes are taught in English. At first, Mum and Dad wanted me to concentrate on the subjects everyone learned back home, like English, Maths and Science. I never took any proper Chinese classes, so look what's happened. Here I am, looking like a pre-schooler.

'Come on,' says Alin, one of the Chinese girls at school. 'You must know how to write the word *Zhongguo*.'

Zhongguo means China. And no, I have no clue how to write it. But when Alin draws two little pictures in the sandy ground, like this –

中国

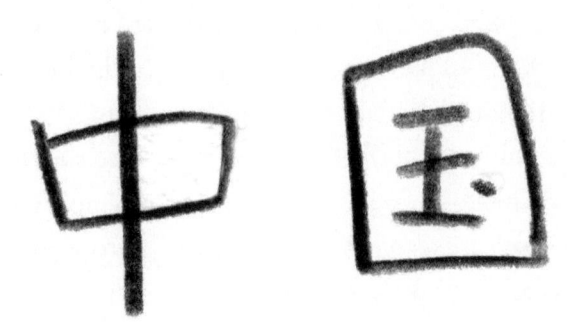

– I vaguely recognize the characters. That's a start.

I can see Alin and her friends laughing. It's easy for them. Their parents are Chinese, but they go to the International School with me and learn English, just as I do. I usually like playing with them. We skip ropes or hop on one leg, counting in Chinese until one of us stumbles or falls over.

I also play 'It' like I did before in England, or 'Capture the Flag' which is popular in America, or 'Land and Water' – a game a girl from India taught me when I first came to the International School – but everything seems so different this year. Last year, whatever game I played, Abby and Laura were always part of it. But they went back to Edinburgh and Chicago before the summer holidays and I still feel upset that they're gone. When I told Mum, she reminded me that most children at the International

School are only here for a certain amount of time – that people leaving was to be expected and that I shouldn't get too attached to anyone. Great advice. How do you not get attached? Abby and Laura were my best friends.

'Try being a good friend to a new kid,' Dad suggested on the first day back at school. He always oversimplifies things. At least, that's what Mum says. I ignored his suggestion at first, but now it pops back into my head. I will find a new person and make their day. It will be as easy as pie. Won't it?

Chapter Two

Our school is right in the bustling, hectic financial centre of Beijing. I stand in the middle of the big, concrete courtyard, surrounded by classrooms. When I look up and turn around, I can see high-rise buildings in every direction. Today feels bright and clear and the perfect time for a fresh start.

Scanning the courtyard, I see some boys on the climbing frame, which is freshly painted in a shocking orange colour. A group of smaller kids are trying to do cartwheels. They all roll around, looking like little penguins falling on top of each other.

Jonas, light-blond and freckled, is sorting out baseball cards with his friends. The Chinese girls from my class are still in the garden, drawing on the ground; the boys are getting ready for a game of football – all but one of them. His name is Weiting and he's new to the school.

Weiting hasn't spoken a single word in class yet. He sits in the last row and is so quiet that the teachers and everyone else overlook him. Anyone would feel miserable and lonely back there. It does, however, make Weiting the perfect target for my friendship mission.

Right now, Weiting is sitting on the wooden bench by the entrance to the sports hall. He's wearing a blue and grey checked shirt. In his hands he's holding a book, but I can see that he's staring through the pages into the space in front of him.

'What are you reading?' I ask as I sit down next to him.

He's clearly surprised and tries to cover the book with his hands. I can see that it's our History textbook, proving he was just pretending to read. Who would read a textbook during break time?

'Nothing,' he says.

'I'm Paulina,' I say, but he just stares ahead, clutching the book. 'I'm in your class,' I continue.

After a short silence, Weiting closes his book. Before he can get up and leave, I say quickly, 'I've been living in Beijing for five years. My mum and dad are both lecturers at the university. At first, we only planned to stay for a year, but then we all really enjoyed it. Can you believe we're still here?'

A bird has landed on the tree behind us and I look up into the rustling leaves to see if I can identify it. 'It would be strange to go back home now. We're from a small town close to Manchester. In the last winter holiday we went back for two weeks and everything seemed too quiet and peaceful. At night I lay in my bed and missed all the sounds of Beijing – the cars, the people, the music.' I glance at Weiting. 'Weird, right?'

Weiting looks at me, squinting because the sun is shining in his face. 'You think it's noisy here? You should see the place where I come from.' His voice is far stronger than I imagined. He gets up, still clutching the textbook tightly to his chest, and walks away.

'Nice to talk to you,' I call, but he doesn't even turn around. 'That went well,' I whisper to myself as he vanishes through the door of the sports hall.

Chapter Three

A lovely smell lingers in the apartment when I open the door. Mum is cooking a curry. As I breathe in, the strong spices tickle my nose.

'Who's coming for dinner?' I shout. Curry is something Mum always cooks when we have visitors. You can just make a huge amount of it, she says, and it will feed everyone.

'It's a surprise!' she calls back from the kitchen and I can tell from her voice that she's excited.

I take off my shoes and put on a pair of slippers before going to my room to get changed. The marble floor of the apartment is cold, even in the summer. It's fun to glide on it in slippers, pretending it's an ice rink.

The apartment's tiny, though. The kitchen opens into the living room. Down the hall, Mum and Dad's bedroom is opposite mine. The apartments on the other side of the road completely block the view from their window.

On my side of the building, I can see the city, with its rectangular towers rising into the sky wherever I look. They're prettiest at night. In the distance I can see the hills outside Beijing. When we have visitors from England, we drive out there to see part of the Great Wall of China. The Wall is beautiful. It's as broad as a street on the top, and you can stand there and see its path winding through hills and mountains for miles on end.

'Paulina, come and say hello,' shouts Mum.

I leave my room, and in the hallway discover a man holding an enormous bunch of flowers, with a woman and a girl standing next to him. I haven't seen the man and woman before, but of course I've seen the girl.

She's new in my grade, though not in my class. It would be impossible to overlook her. Everything about her is fabulous, from her dark blue eyes to the way she holds her chin up. She's wearing skinny jeans and a short pink top with sequins that match the band that sparkles in her shiny black hair.

She examines me curiously. Only then do I realize that, out of pure habit, I've already put on my pyjama trousers. They are nice and soft, made from navy blue silk, but there's a small hole in them, showing the skin above my knee.

Why didn't Mum tell me that a girl from my school was coming, not her boring work friends? I really would have dressed up a bit.

'You won't believe it,' Mum says with the excited, happy smile in her eyes that is usually reserved for birthday mornings and chocolate cakes. 'This is my old friend, Susan, from university. We'd completely lost touch until I saw her at school this morning.'

'Susan, Tim and Zoe have just moved here,' continues Dad, giving the man called Tim a nudge on the shoulder. 'But you must have met Zoe at school given you're the same age.'

Zoe shakes her head vigorously, so I just say, 'I think Zoe is in the other class.'

'I'm so excited,' says Mum. 'It's just wonderful to unexpectedly find an old friend again.'

Susan smiles at me kindly. 'Your mum told me all about you and how well you cope with living abroad. I only hope that Zoe makes the transition as well as you did. I can imagine it's not always easy.'

'Oh no,' I say. 'I love living here. Beijing is so exciting. I never get bored.'

'That's the spirit,' says Tim. 'We hope that you can tell Zoe all about it. She's missing her friends back home in England a lot.'

I nod my head and smile at Zoe. She turns around and frowns at her dad.

'Come on, Paulina,' says Dad. 'Show Zoe your room. You still have half an hour until dinner.'

I walk ahead and open the door to my room but when I look back to see if Zoe has followed, she is still standing close to her mum, not moving in the slightest. Her mum gives her a little push and she stumbles reluctantly down the hall and through my bedroom door.

Chapter Four

My room is simply too small for all my stuff, which means that it sometimes looks a little bit messy. It isn't messy today, though. I guess Mum must have cleaned up before I came home.

I sit down on my bed, next to the navy cushion with an embroidered phoenix threaded in bright red yarn. Dad and I bought it at a night-market on my first evening out in Beijing. It always reminds me of the excitement I felt that night: the throngs of people, or *ren shan ren hai* – a sea of people – as the Chinese would say; everyone pushing slowly through small, dimly lit alleys, revelling in the colourful displays of seafood and exotic fruit and breathing in the mouth-watering scents of the food being prepared on the little stalls all around – fried noodles, roast duck, pancakes and countless other delicacies.

Zoe inspects my room; the expression on her face gives nothing away. She looks at the pile of cuddly toys on the far side of my bed, at my desk covered with books and papers and a scatter of colourful felt-tip pens. She stares at the little plastic carousel hanging over my desk where I keep my socks on pegs.

I have a basket of plastic dolls in one corner of the room, also mostly bought by Dad and me at the night-markets.

They're different from English dolls. Most of them are soft and squishy, and their clothes have funny details, like lots of yellow ribbons or oversized sleeves. Zoe moves toward the basket and pulls out a doll wearing a red Chinese wedding dress.

'Do you play with these?' she asks. Without thinking I nod, but before I can explain that I collect the dolls, rather than actually play with them, Zoe turns her attention to my wardrobe.

The wardrobe is old and wooden and has the double happiness sign painted on it –

囍

– which is the only Chinese character I can recognize without thinking, probably because it is in front of my nose every day. Zoe fingers the carving.

'It's a Chinese character and means double happiness. When you get married, people give you cards and furniture and lots of other things with this sign on it – even wardrobes,' I explain.

'So how come you've got one when you're not married?' asks Zoe as she opens the doors of the wardrobe. Mum clearly has not cleaned up in there. The piles of clothes that were lying on my bed and floor this morning have been stuffed into the wardrobe in a big lumpy pile. I feel my cheeks getting hot.

'My parents bought it for me,' I say. 'Oh, talking about weddings, I do have a traditional Chinese dress that I could wear at a wedding.' I jump up and walk over. Luckily, I know exactly where my *qipao* is hanging.

'See,' I say, pulling the soft purple silken dress with the high collar out of the wardrobe and quickly shutting the doors. 'We went to a special tailor to have it made.'

Zoe takes the hem of the dress between two fingers to feel its fabric. 'Looks like the ones they sell on the street,' she says, turning away with a shrug.

'No!' I say with mild indignation. 'Can't you feel how soft the silk is?' But Zoe has already discovered something else. Her eyes are resting on a small roll of Chinese paper with two characters, drawn in thick black ink.

'My name,' I say, smiling. 'To be honest, it's more of a joke. My Chinese name is Sun Baoli; our class teacher picked it for me when I started school here. But before I had a proper Chinese name, Mum and Dad's colleagues called me *baobei*. That means baby, but people also use it to say darling.'

'*Baobei*?' Zoe repeats mockingly, raising an eyebrow.

'Yes,' I nod, although her pronunciation isn't very clear.

'Whatever,' says Zoe. 'I'm starving. What's for dinner?'

'Mum's cooking curry,' I explain. 'It isn't too spicy and doesn't have too many vegetables in it. Don't worry.'

Zoe frowns. 'I see,' she says. 'Do you have anything else in the meantime?'

I grin and take out the cardboard box from under my bed. 'Secret stash,' I say. 'You should try the egg rolls. They're biscuits and taste simply delicious. If I open any of the dried fish Mum will smell it right away. She gets really cross if I eat before dinner.'

'Dried fish?' asked Zoe. 'Do you seriously eat that?'

'I know it sounds disgusting but once you've tried it, you can't stop eating it. Believe me. Maybe after dinner?'

I hold out an egg roll biscuit to Zoe, but she doesn't take it. Instead, she points at the poster over my bed. 'Who's that?' she asks.

'One of my favourite Chinese singers. Have you heard any Mandarin pop yet?'

Zoe looks puzzled and shakes her head. Before she can say another word, I run outside and ask Dad for the laptop. Luckily he can't really say no with guests around.

As fast as I can, I rush back to my room, determined to give Zoe the best introduction to Chinese culture ever.

Chapter Five

While Zoe looks at the screen with a bored expression, I remember how I felt when I first watched Mandarin pop videos. 'Did you hear that?' I ask Zoe eagerly. 'He sang *wo ai ni* which means "I love you." The melodies and the lyrics can be totally cheesy, but it's like the dried fish. I can't stop eating that, and I can't stop listening to these songs now.'

The clip I show her next is a new one, and I move my lips silently to the words, which I already know off by heart. Zoe watches me almost as much as she looks at the screen, which is a little unnerving. I'm quite glad when Dad knocks on the door to tell us dinner's ready.

'Enough screen time,' announces Dad, ushering us into the living room. As we're leaving the bedroom, Zoe turns round to me. 'Who's your favourite English singer?' she asks. I try to think of someone, but no one immediately comes to mind.

The food is set on the round, wooden Chinese dinner table. Mum, Dad, Susan and Tim are already sitting down, talking about people I don't know. Dad indicates the two free chairs and Zoe sits down on one of them quietly. She curls a strand of hair around her finger, looks at the ceiling, and completely ignores the food.

'You should really try the curry,' I say after a few minutes, but Zoe just pushes her plate away. Her silence is starting to worry me, but neither Mum nor Dad nor Zoe's parents seem to notice. After dinner, Mum and Susan relax on the sofa, with Dad and Tim on the armchairs either side of them. The coffee table is full of little treats and I can't help exclaiming, 'Sour plums and shrimp crackers – my favourite!'

'There are also chocolates, Zoe,' says Mum. 'Not everyone shares Paulina's tastes,' she smiles.

'Only millions of Chinese children,' I reply with my mouth full. One look at the clock tells me that it is time for my new favourite TV programme. I beg Mum and Dad to switch it on, but they insist that the no-TV-with-visitors policy still stands.

I'm a bit surprised when Zoe says very quietly, 'I'd like to see what Paulina likes to watch. Is it a game show?'

Before I can answer, Mum says, 'It is indeed. The competitors travel through China and take part in challenges along the way. It's quite funny, though sometimes I find it rather silly. But then, I don't understand most of it.'

'It's meant to be silly,' I explain. 'That's what makes it fun.'

In the end, the TV stays off. It doesn't matter too much, since I always record it anyway. I'll just watch it tomorrow.

Tim and Susan have thousands of questions about school. Which teachers do I like? What's my favourite subject? What's the food like? While I talk and make the grown-ups laugh with my stories, I see Zoe's face glazing over. I feel sorry for her. She clearly doesn't want to be here.

At last, Mum realizes the same thing. 'How about you, Zoe?' she says. 'Why don't you tell us your first impressions after a week of school?'

'Everything seems really easy,' says Zoe. 'I've covered most of the subjects at home already. And it's a shame there are hardly any sports lessons.'

Tim and Susan exchange a worried look.

'Zoe really likes sports,' says Susan. 'It's usually the other subjects ... '

'Mum!' hisses Zoe, before Susan can finish her sentence.

Tim looks at his watch. 'I can't believe it's so late already. We should really go now.'

Zoe has already got up from the sofa, while Mum protests, 'It's the weekend! Please stay a little longer. How about a cup of tea?'

But Zoe is already standing by the front door. I follow her.

'It was great that you came tonight,' I smile. 'So, I guess we'll see each other on Monday at school.'

Zoe looks at me smirkingly, twirling her curls with her forefinger, the other hand resting on the door handle. In a cold voice she says, 'Can't wait.'

Chapter Six

At first, it seems to be just another ordinary Monday morning. We have an assembly and the head teacher hands out certificates for last year's best music performances. She mistakenly calls out Laura's name, then puts her certificate quickly behind the others and moves on.

It feels a bit like a stab in the stomach, being reminded of my friend. I look around, half-hoping to see her, but knowing this is impossible. Two rows behind me, I suddenly spot Zoe. She's wearing a soft, cuddly-looking light-blue jumper. I smile at her and wave, but she looks right through me. My stomach really hurts now.

We have English and Science for the first two lessons of the day. English is OK, because we're still writing about our summer holidays and thinking back to the days I spent on the beach at Hainan Island with Mum and Dad makes me happy. For Science we join the other class in the laboratory, and this is when I first realize that something is wrong. Last week, Ellie from the other class really wanted to pair up with me. Three or four of her friends had left school before the summer and we talked about how she missed them. Actually, we talked and giggled a bit too much, so Mrs Kramer, the Science teacher, got quite cross with us.

Ellie is already in the laboratory with most of her class, preparing her workstation, when I enter. I walk straight over to her and say, 'Hi, can I join you again?' and place my books on the desk.

'I think,' she says, looking around, 'Zoe wanted to work with me today.'

'Exactly.' I can hear a voice behind me. 'You don't mind, do you – *Baobei*?' Zoe says, as she picks up my books from Ellie's desk and hands them back to me.

Alin and her friends giggle.

'No,' I mumble, turning around.

There is only one free space, next to Weiting in the last row. He's on his own. I don't even ask if I can join him. I just put my books on the desk without a word and start sorting out our equipment.

At lunchtime things get even weirder. Whenever I walk past any of my classmates, they start whispering. Heads together; all I can see is their backs. Trying to talk to people doesn't make it better either. Nina says she has no clue about our English homework and runs away. Shanshan just gives me a nasty glare when I ask her if table tennis is on after school. And then, of course, there is Zoe. She's everywhere today. In front of our English classroom, giggling with some girls from my class, only to stop talking when I walk past. Then in the courtyard, glancing over at me as she laughs with Arianne, and again among the Chinese girls under the trees, rolling her eyes and making big dramatic gestures.

'You shouldn't worry about her,' says a voice behind me. 'I know the type. She'll lose interest in you soon enough. Any intelligent person will figure out that she's talking nonsense.'

It's Weiting. He has his hands in his jeans pockets and looks exhausted after such a long speech.

'What's she saying?' I ask immediately.

'Nonsense,' he replies, already heading back inside.

* * *

Lunch break seems extra long today. I have no idea where to go or who to play with. Finally, to avoid Zoe's presence, I walk into the library. It's quiet in here. Apart from Luowen, who is scribbling what might be extra homework in a book, no other students are around.

I stand in front of a shelf, but my eyes can't focus. The book spines look like nothing but coloured stripes with dots on them.

'Can I help you, dear?'

Next to me stands Mrs Lundman, the dark-haired librarian. She has very red lips and a strong Swedish accent.

I find it hard to answer.

'Let's sit down,' she suggests, and the next moment I am sitting on the comfy green leather sofa next to her desk.

'There are two kinds of visitors to the library during lunch break,' she says.

I look blank.

'Let me explain. First, there are the children who always have their head in a book.' She points her chin slightly in Luowen's direction. 'I don't blame them – they just can't resist it. Actually, I was one of them when I was young. Then,' she looks at me, 'there are the ones that I rarely see in here, apart from library lessons.' Her voice turns very soft and she comes a bit closer. 'Some of them come here for a few days, others for weeks in a row. That doesn't matter. The important thing is, eventually they stop coming during lunch break. They go back to whatever they used to do at break time before.'

I take a deep breath. Mrs Lundman evidently doesn't expect me to say anything because she just continues talking. 'Now, I have one more grain of wisdom to share with you. Did you know that you can find the answer to any question in the world in a book?'

'Like in an encyclopedia?' I ask.

She laughs in a deep voice. 'No, almost never in an encyclopedia. How about you try this one for a start?'

She pulls out a thick volume with a torn cover showing a girl fighting a dragon. Ten minutes later, I'm engaged in a medieval family feud, and I forget all about Zoe until the bell rings.

Chapter Seven

The afternoon is a bit better than the morning. I am so busy with my lessons that I hardly have time to talk to anyone. All the teachers seem to agree that they have big plans for us this year. At least, that's their excuse for giving us so much homework.

When I get home, I open up my English book and try to concentrate on the features of a non-chronological report on water plants, but whenever I look at the blank pages, Zoe's face pops up in my head. What has happened to make her act so weird? Did I do something wrong that evening when she came to visit? Zoe certainly isn't shy around other people. In fact, everyone seems to be fascinated by her. How could she have made so many friends at school so quickly? I tap my lips with my pen. What has Zoe told the other kids about me? Was Weiting right about her? Would Zoe stop talking about me if I didn't pay any attention to her?

'Mum?' I say, waiting until she takes off her reading glasses to look at me. 'Can we please go to the park? I could do some sketching there to add to my report.'

Mum hesitates for a moment, glancing at the papers spread out on the desk in front of her. 'Sure,' she says. 'I'll just sort out some work to take with me.'

Ritan Park is only a few blocks away from our apartment and it has been my playground ever since we moved to Beijing. It's a huge space with loads of things to do. I'm too old for the actual playground now, but I still go on the climbing wall. Mum and I often spend our afternoons here, with me reading a book while Mum catches up with some of her work.

When you walk under the drooping willows and look at the winding canals and the lake with its dark green water and lily pads, it feels like walking in an Asian fairy tale. It is not too crowded today, which is a good thing, since I can wander around and look in peace for some interesting water plants to draw.

A group of old ladies are sitting around a picnic table, playing *mah-jong*, a Chinese board game. It is one of those games only grown-ups enjoy. Too many rules, too complicated and too much waiting around for my taste.

'Hey, Paulina,' I hear someone calling.

It's Mrs Shen, our neighbour, who used to babysit me. Her children have moved out and she says her husband is too boring to spend too much time with so she comes to Ritan Park every day. She waves at me with a blue and white fan. She's in a group of other women and men who are all practising a martial art.

At first, I couldn't believe that anyone could defend themselves with just a fan, but it's traditional in China.

Once people master it, it looks really beautiful.

Now Mrs Shen waves frantically at me, but I don't want to join in and mouth, '*buyao, xiexie*' to her. That means, 'I don't want to, thank you.'

Mum has found a bench nearby and is already deeply buried in her work. What I want is a nice calm spot where I can have my thoughts to myself, with a good view of one of the ponds. Once I've made myself comfortable on a patch of grass, leaning my back against a smooth, light-grey rock, I stare into the sky, then close my eyes. My sketch book is on my lap and my pencil almost slips out of my hand.

It would be so nice to have Abby or Laura next to me now. We would make silly jokes and take turns drawing each other's faces. Just thinking about it makes me smile.

Suddenly, I can feel something warm close to my right hand. It is only the tiniest sensation, but it makes me open my eyes. At first, I'm startled, but I try to keep as still as possible.

Next to my hand sits a tortoise. It is almost as big as my sketch book and, funnily enough, its shell is the same olive colour. I've never seen a tortoise roaming around in the park before.

The tortoise seems to be interested in my pencil, because it keeps its head very close to it. Slowly, it starts to raise its head and I could swear its intense red eyes with pitch-black pupils are studying my face.

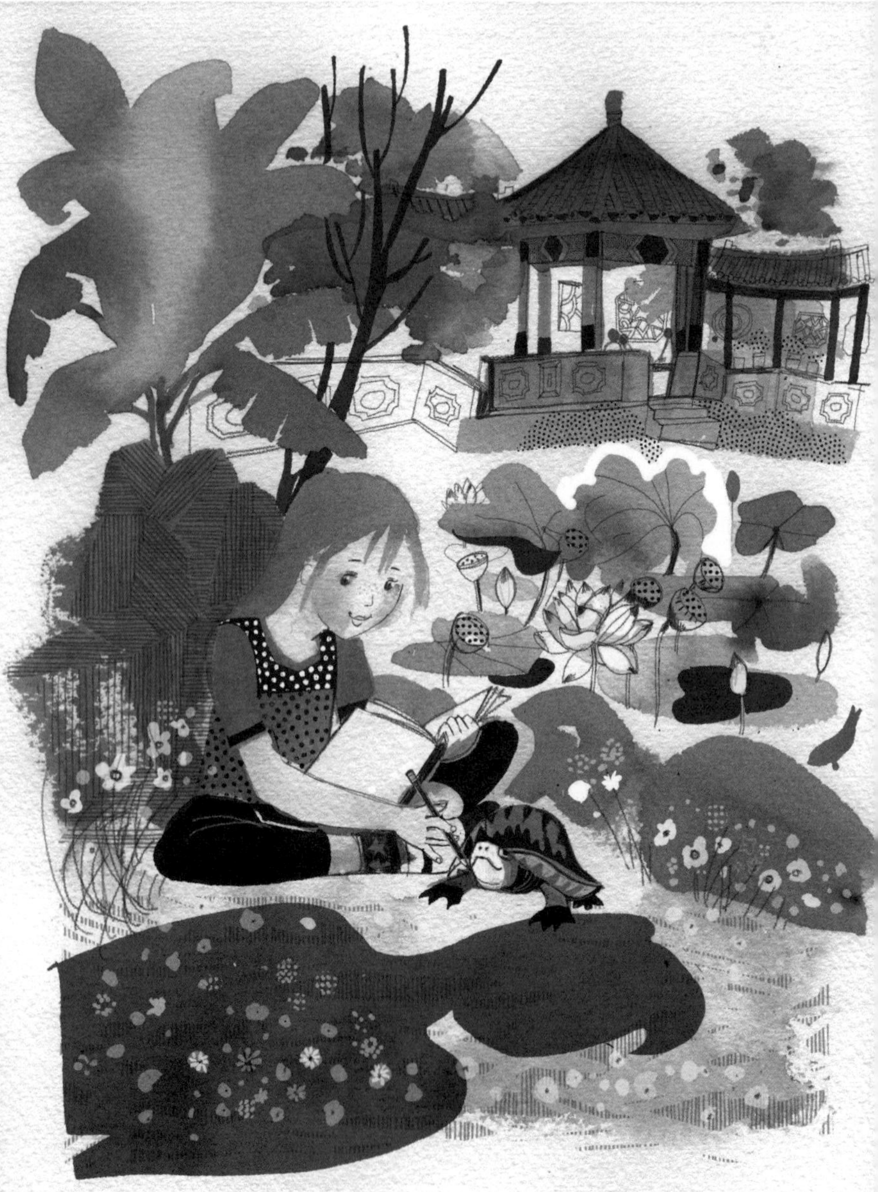

Suddenly I drop my pencil, because a voice just over my head is saying, 'So this is where you're hiding, you little beast!' Then the voice says more calmly, 'Paulina, what are you doing with Xia?'

Chapter Eight

Weiting's shadow falls over my face. He is wearing a stripy hoody and seems totally out of breath, as if he's been running laps around the park.

'Xia – is that its name?' I point with my left hand to the tortoise, who stares at me.

For a few seconds, Weiting doesn't say a word, but the way he pulls his eyebrows together conveys his tension. I wonder why he's always so quiet around me.

Instead of looking me in the eye, he stares at the tortoise.

'He's named after the first Chinese dynasty. *Yeye*, my grandad, claims Xia is almost as old as this country, which of course is not true, just like all his other turtle stories.' He is opening and closing his hands into tight fists. '*Yeye* always gets angry if I can't find the turtle when he wants to go home – as if it's my fault that he lets Xia roam around freely.'

'Isn't he a tortoise rather than a turtle?' I ask.

'*Yeye* says Xia is an American box turtle who ended up on the wrong continent. Maybe you would call him a tortoise in your country.' Then he stops talking and he just looks at me, his eyebrows relaxed now.

'Here you go,' I say, stretching my hands out towards Xia.

'Stop that!' Weiting cries. '*Yeye* gets furious when other

people touch Xia. Can you please wait here with him while I go and get my grandad?'

'With pleasure,' I say in a high, artificial voice which makes Weiting smile.

When he is gone, I slowly lower myself down until I am almost at the turtle's eye-level. He doesn't move, but his eyes follow my movements observantly. Somehow his legs remind me of elephant legs: they are round, like pillars, but flexible and soft with shimmering green scales. It is hard to resist the temptation to touch them.

I push myself back a little, so that I am lying on my tummy, my nose very close to the turtle's face.

'What are you doing now?' Weiting is back. 'Didn't I tell you not to touch him?'

Before I can explain that I haven't touched his precious turtle, I notice an old man standing behind Weiting. He has a shock of white hair and is wearing a dark suit with a white T-shirt underneath. He isn't much taller than Weiting, but he gives me such a sharp look that I scramble to my feet in seconds.

Weiting pulls me to the side. 'Can you listen to me for once?' he asks. 'Now please don't try to talk to my grandad. It seems you talk a lot when you're nervous, and my grandad can't stand that. He can be terribly grumpy. Just let him pick up his turtle.'

I wonder why Weiting is so panicky. I am sure his grandad would be perfectly pleasant if I started to talk to him. Most Chinese people I've met seem to enjoy listening to me speaking their language.

Weiting's grandad walks very slowly in the direction of the turtle, who looks at his owner with knowing eyes. Suddenly, the old man stops. First he bows his head very slowly, then bends his knees, one after the other, finally kneeling in front of the turtle.

Xia is craning his neck forward a bit – or am I imagining it? The old man reaches out with his tanned hands, picks up the turtle on both sides of his shell and cradles him close to his body. Only then does he turn his attention back to Weiting, saying in a gruff voice, 'It must be your lucky day, Grandson.'

How come Weiting's grandad speaks in such a strong Beijing accent? I wonder. *Didn't his family come from Taiwan?* For a moment I really feel I should say something, but I remember Weiting's request.

His grandad walks away, a slight, dark figure with white hair down to his shoulders, but Weiting doesn't follow him.

'You're right,' I say at last, stepping a bit closer to Weiting. 'Your grandad looks even grumpier than you. And, just so you know – I'm not nervous at all.'

Chapter Nine

Mrs Lundman startles me when she sits down on the leather sofa right next to me, holding a pile of books in her hands.

'Sorry, dear,' she says, realizing she must have just forcefully extracted me from between the pages of the expedition story I was reading.

I nod, slightly dazed, and a look at the clock tells me that there is more than half an hour left before I need to show up at my dreaded Maths lesson.

'Paulina,' says Mrs Lundman, carefully adjusting her horn-rimmed glasses with a twinkle in her eyes that suggests she's just had a brilliant idea. 'It is indeed lovely to see you here reading so often. Since you have become such a frequent visitor to the library, do you think I could ask for a favour?'

I blush. Mrs Lundman is very kind, but we both know pretty well why I've become a frequent visitor to the library in the last two weeks: my options of who to spend time with have run out.

'Of course,' I say, forcing a smile.

Mrs Lundman puts the pile of books on the small table in front of us. They are boldly coloured picture books, all written in Chinese. My guess is they're for very small children.

'My problem, Paulina,' says Mrs Lundman, 'is that we are trying to establish a section of Chinese books. We should have done this a while ago, but I have only got as far as collecting the books and keeping them in boxes. It's a bit embarrassing, but I don't read Chinese at all and I'm sure I'd make mistakes if I tried to organize them. So maybe you could have a look at them and help me out? It shouldn't take too long as these are all beginners' books.'

'But I can't read Chinese,' I say, trying to avoid her gaze.

Mrs Lundman looks at me wide-eyed. 'I've heard you talk, Paulina. Everyone says your Chinese is amazing. Even Mr Jenkins, and you know what he's like.'

'Well, I've never really learned to read and write,' I explain. 'There's just no time with all the other school subjects. It's really difficult to study Chinese characters, you know.'

Mrs Lundman pushes down her glasses a bit and purses her red lips.

'Well, how about you ask one of your Chinese friends to help out?'

I feel a big lump forming in my stomach. It's been so many days since I've talked properly to someone at school. How can I just go and ask for a favour now?

'You still have half an hour,' says Mrs Lundman, handing me the books. 'Go and see if you can find someone to help.'

The sun is shining brightly down on the courtyard. It is a beautiful autumn day, but that doesn't help me at all. Slowly, I walk towards the sycamore trees, where Alin and four of her friends are playing the sand game. All of them are holding small sticks in their hands, and a girl with two amazingly long plaits is writing in the sand.

It seems like an eternity until I reach them, and Alin only shoots me a short glance before she turns back to the game.

'Alin?' I say. Everyone stops playing and looks at me, apart from the girl with the plaits, who is too absorbed in whatever she is scribbling in the sand. I take a deep breath to keep my voice from trembling. 'I was wondering if you could help me with something. It's a job for Mrs Lundman, but I can't do it on my own, because I can't read Chinese.'

I wonder how I even manage to say these words. Alin used to tease me about not being able to write, and that was before Zoe persuaded everyone to ostracize me.

'Right,' says Alin, looking like a police inspector about to arrest a criminal. 'You seriously think I'm going to help you, after all you've said?' Two of the other girls start whispering and I can hear the word 'outrageous'.

'What do you mean?' I ask, gripping the books tightly.

'It seems there are a lot of things you don't like here, apart from reading and writing Chinese,' says Alin, chin jutting forward and both hands on her hips.

'I have no idea what you're talking about,' I say.

'How about our silly jokes and soppy music?'

My head feels hot and I start to lose my grip on the books. What on earth has Zoe told them? My mouth is so dry I can't even open it, and the only thing I want to do is run away. So that's exactly what I do: I turn around and start to sprint, squeezing the books as if they could help me escape faster.

All the way across the courtyard I run, towards the Science building, one flight down the stairs, to the only safe space I can imagine – the space I always shared with Abby and Laura.

All I want is to crouch in the tiny space under the stairs, where the cleaners store their supplies. Behind a vacuum cleaner and a floor polisher and lots of bottles of detergent lies the old rug where I used to sit with Abby and Laura, when we wanted to be sure that nobody could listen in to our conversations – the place where we used to console each other after an exam went wrong, or when we lost to the French school in a football match.

My eyes are so watery that I don't realize I'm not alone. In fact, before I see him I almost fall on top of him, as I plunge down to the floor, out of breath, sweaty and very shaky.

He shouts so loudly that I bang my head on the back of one of the lower stairs, trying to get away from him. Only then do we recognize each other.

'Where on earth do I have to go to get away from you?' asks Weiting in his usual grumpy tone. Then he seems to change his mind. 'What's wrong?'

I don't know where to start. What Zoe has done is only slowly starting to sink in. All those things I said about cheesy music and silly jokes and the foods that sound weird when you first hear about them ... I thought she understood that I like all those things; in fact, I really love them. But why would Zoe run around school telling stories to all my friends, getting things completely the wrong way round? And why would everyone believe her?

While I've been chewing my lip, Weiting has picked up the books that were scattered all around us.

'I know this story,' he says. '"The Frog in the Well" – *jing di zhi wa*. I must have read it a hundred times when I was little.'

And then he reads out the story to me. He sounds so different from the people in Beijing, whose accents are hard and throaty. It feels like I'm listening to a song.

When he's finished, he points at the title:

井底之蛙

'Now you read,' he says. 'You know, you have the funniest accent for a foreigner. You sound like a mixture of my grandad and someone from an American TV show.'

'I can't,' I say, a blush rising to my face. The last thing I want to do today is talk about me not being English *or* Chinese enough.

Weiting pulls out a piece of paper and a pen from his backpack. He draws on it. Two horizontal lines and two vertical lines. '*Jing*,' he says. '"A well" – look at the first character on the cover.'

井

It is totally easy to spot. I can identify characters if you show them to me, but I don't seem to be able to keep them in my mind. And of course, I can't write them. 'There's a special order to write the strokes in,' I say, half to myself. 'It's complicated.'

'I thought you'd be exactly the type of person who loves "complicated". Writing Chinese characters should be just your thing,' chuckles Weiting.

'Well,' I say after a while, considering his words, 'actually, I'd like to ask you a favour.'

Weiting tilts his head to the side and studies my face. 'It depends,' he says.

'I do need help with these books. I'm actually doing a job for Mrs Lundman. She's asked me to sort out the Chinese books.'

'I thought you couldn't read Chinese,' he says.

'Exactly. So that's where you come in.'

He gets up, gathering up his school books and putting his lunch box into his backpack. 'I guess I could help,' he says. 'Especially after you helped me find that turtle the other day.'

Upstairs a door opens and the sound of many trampling feet makes it hard to hear him. Weiting holds out a hand in my direction and while I shake it to seal the deal he says, 'But in return, you have to start learning to write Chinese.

Otherwise, who will sort out the books when I'm gone?'

I honestly hope that Weiting doesn't return to Taiwan too soon. Because right now, he's the only friend I've got.

Chapter Ten

Under my bed lies a little grey exercise book with pages so thin they are almost transparent. On each page are one hundred little squares, spaced out over ten lines. In the first square of each line is a Chinese character, while the following nine are empty for me to practise my own writing in.

Weiting has the neatest, most painstaking handwriting that never shows any sign of hesitation. On top of each character, he's written the pronunciation and the English meaning of the word. He's decorated each character with little numbers and tiny arrows to show me how to write it.

I learned thirty-five characters last week and was pretty proud of myself until Weiting told me that the goal should be at least fifty characters per week. That would bring me to two hundred characters in a month and after approximately two years ... I might be able to read a newspaper.

Weiting always points out that he won't be here for long, so I'd better hurry up and try to learn one hundred characters in a week. One hundred! He does have a strange sense of humour, but I'm getting used to it. I didn't even complain when he made me learn two very complicated Chinese characters that make up the word 'basketball' – *lanqiu* – in the first week. I know now that basketball is Weiting's favourite sport:

籃球

At least all this learning keeps me busy at break time now. First, we spend twenty minutes in the library, where Mrs Lundman always waits for us with some biscuits and a secretive smile, as if Weiting and I are on a mysterious mission and not just sorting out a few Chinese children's books. Then we go to the hiding place under the stairs and Weiting looks at the writing I've done at home.

I'm almost enjoying break time at the moment, but whenever I try to talk to Weiting about anything but Chinese characters, he goes very quiet. I've tried asking him about his grandad and the turtle, but he just repeats the same thing – that they are both stubborn creatures and I shouldn't be bothered about them at all.

Just as I'm wondering whether it's time to start writing in my exercise book, my bedroom door suddenly opens – Mum never knocks.

She comes in and sits down on my bed looking tired from all the research work she's been doing. Dad says she's working through most of the night too, and by her side of the bed I've seen mountains of books about Chinese history.

'What are you doing?' she asks.

'Not much,' I say. 'Weiting is still teaching me to write Chinese.'

Mum and Dad didn't make a fuss when I announced I was finally going to start learning Chinese characters, but I saw the excitement in the glances they exchanged.

'Can we have a quick chat?' she asks, and a lot of tiny wrinkles around her eyes indicate that this is a worried smile.

'Sure.'

'You know we went to your parents' evening last night, don't you?'

I nod, although actually I had forgotten.

'Well, it was nothing out of the ordinary, in case you were wondering. It's very early in the school year.' After a little pause, she adds, 'The only thing is that Mrs Wen wanted to have a word with me and Dad. Paulina, is something bothering you at school?'

'No,' I lie, trying to ignore the little knots forming in my stomach. 'It's just that it always takes a while to get used to school again after the holidays.'

'I understand.' Mum strokes my hair and I can smell the ink of her books on her hands. 'It must be tricky, now both Abby and Laura have gone. Mrs Wen thinks you should try to make some new friends. To put it in her words – "Paulina looks so lonely."'

'I *have* made new friends,' I say quickly. 'There's Weiting.'

'Of course,' Mum says. 'It's lovely that he's teaching you Chinese now. But I still think we should invite Zoe over again soon. Maybe we could all go on a day trip together.'

'No, Mum. Not Zoe,' I say, as the knots in my stomach turn into a gigantic, writhing lump. 'Please.'

Mum stops stroking my hair. 'That's not very kind,' she says. 'There's more to Zoe than meets the eye. Believe me, she really needs our support. Just imagine if you were the new girl. If you don't want to make an effort to help her, could you do it as a favour for me? I'm so happy to have Susan and Tim here. It would be amazing if you girls could get along together.'

Dad's call from the living room interrupts us, so Mum

leaves me, and suddenly I'm not in the mood for writing any more.

Chapter Eleven

Weiting hasn't been at school for the last three days and I'm wondering what's wrong with him. On Monday at break time, I rushed off to the library, only to find the door closed with a notice pinned to it, declaring that Mrs Lundman was attending a seminar for a whole week – which meant the library would be closed until her return.

So today, Wednesday, I'm spending lunchtime all on my own for the third time. When I get to the lunch hall, almost all the spaces are taken. I'm standing between the tables, scanning the room for a spot where I can eat my rice and vegetables peacefully. It's hopeless. The only free seat is at Alin's table and we haven't spoken since the incident under the trees. While I'm still wondering where to sit, someone calls me. It's Zoe.

'Hey, *Baobei*, come and sit with us.' She smiles smugly and pushes up the sleeves of the navy sweater that makes her look so grown-up. Everyone's looking at me, trying to figure out what I will do. My only options are to run away and forget about lunch altogether, or to join the others and hope that Zoe has changed her mind about me.

In a very bossy way she pulls the empty chair next to Alin towards her and forces the other girls on the neighbouring table to make space for me. Hesitantly, I lower my tray and sit down between Zoe and Manon, staring at the other five girls from my grade, the usual crew that hangs around with Zoe.

'Are you a vegetarian?' Manon asks. I shake my head, trying to pick up the cabbage and rice on my fork. 'Why aren't you having the meatballs, then?'

One look around tells me that all of Zoe's friends have chosen pasta and meatballs today.

Zoe giggles. 'Because she isn't used to this kind of food any more,' she says, making everyone laugh out loud.

Manon doesn't stop. 'Is it true that you don't know any English singers?'

Zoe's high laughter and the other girls' giggles swallow my answer. My cheeks stinging, I start to bolt my food and ignore the rest of their talk. The last thing I want is for them to see they're upsetting me. It's the worst feeling to sit in a crowd feeling so alone.

* * *

It's four o'clock, and since Mum is too busy to leave the house, she's asked Mrs Shen to accompany me to the park today. The air outside is still warm, but the slightly cooler breeze I feel on my cheeks tells me that autumn is almost here. I'm watching Mrs Shen and three of her friends doing the fan exercise, while an old Chinese folk song plays on a radio. It's busier than usual here today, but despite all the people walking, playing and talking all around me, it feels wonderfully peaceful and safe.

After sitting calmly on a bench for a few minutes, I get the feeling that someone is watching me. I look around, but everyone's minding their own business, none of them interested in me.

For some reason I glance under the bench. And there he is, staring at me with his red and black eyes, curious and indifferent at the same time.

'Xia,' I say, but before I can stretch out my hand to touch him, a voice above my head raps out sharply: '*Bie dong* – don't move.'

It is Weiting's grandad. He is dressed in the same black suit as last time, but now the T-shirt underneath is bright purple. I can't tell how old he is exactly, but the way he suddenly squats, stretching out his hand to the turtle, makes him seem like a young man.

The turtle and Weiting's grandad have made eye contact and, just like last time, Xia seems to give a little signal with his eyes, the tiniest of winks, that allows the old man to pick him up. They look like good friends to me.

Then both of them turn and rest their eyes on me:

one pair full of curiosity, the other full of irritation.

Weiting's grandad is already turning around to leave, which would probably be best for all of us, but I can't stop myself saying, 'It really wasn't my fault. Not this time and not the last time. Xia just seems to find me.'

Weiting's grandad faces me again and I can see now that he looks more curious than annoyed. 'What is your name?' he asks.

'Sun Baoli,' I answer, swearing secretly to myself that I will never make the baby joke again.

'Sun *xiaojie*,' says Weiting's grandad, in a rather formal manner. It means 'Miss' Sun. I'm surprised that he is treating me like an adult for once. 'I am Han Weigang.'

Very slowly, he walks to the other edge of the bench and takes a seat, letting his eyes wander through the park. Between the two of us there is enough space for at least two more people. From a distance, Mrs Shen is watching us and waving at me to check everything is OK. I give her a thumbs up.

'So, where is—?' I start, but Mr Han puts a finger to his lips and shushes me. Carefully, he puts Xia down on the bench facing him. The turtle's head retreats halfway back into his shell, but then Xia seems to relax and stretches out his neck again.

We are both watching Xia and it's almost as if the noise around us slowly fades away, just as it does sometimes in a movie when the main character concentrates on something important.

For a turtle, Xia's movements are very graceful, without any pauses or hesitations. I'm not sure how long it takes for him to turn around, but once he has changed direction, he starts moving towards me, one thick leg after the other in a seamless, steady motion until he has arrived right by my side.

'Fascinating,' says Mr Han.

Chapter Twelve

For a few minutes we sit silently, both our gazes fixed on the turtle and his gleaming red eyes. The voices of the visitors and the sounds of the park have receded even further away now, as if they don't belong here at all.

'Tell me, Miss Sun, are you enjoying the peacefulness of the park?' Mr Han's voice sounds much friendlier now.

I'm tempted to politely make small talk with him, but there's something much more important on my mind.

'Where is Weiting?' I ask.

The smile fades from Mr Han's face. In front of us a toddler is chasing his ball, kicking it right to Mr Han's feet. Instead of picking it up and handing it to the child, he kicks it away angrily. I jump up, manage to get the ball and hand it to the little boy.

'So, where is he?' I say, sitting back down next to Xia. Xia's only visible body part now is his shell, with its marks that look like the ancient bark of a giant tree.

'At home,' Mr Han grumbles, 'being indulged by his parents, who tell me he has a fever and needs a rest. If you ask me, I'd say he's making it up.'

'He's making up a fever?' I ask incredulously.

Mr Han doesn't attempt to answer, instead taking an interest in my exercise book. 'How are your studies going?' he asks.

So Weiting must have told him about teaching me the characters. 'I'm still finding it difficult,' I reply. 'There are just too many Chinese characters to learn. It will take me years!'

'Not years,' he exclaims. 'This is a lifelong study – that's what makes it so interesting. Can you believe that I still don't know the meaning of some characters? I don't think any human being can keep them all in their mind.'

As I nod politely, I spot Mrs Shen signalling to me. She wants to leave, but Mr Han has grabbed my book. He starts scanning through the pages, obviously unimpressed. On a blank page, he starts writing characters at enormous speed and doesn't stop until he has written at least fifty of them.

'You remember the character for goal or ambition?' he asks me.

I haven't learned that yet, so I shake my head.

'My daughter gave me this pen, as if anything could replace ink and a paintbrush,' he mumbles. A brush pen appears in his tanned, wrinkled hands and he writes in one of the little squares in my book:

志

'See the upper part is "a scholar", the lower part is "the heart". Now, you might think that this is very romantic, but in ancient China, we thought that the heart was actually the brain. It all got a bit muddled up in later centuries, but whatever the scholar wants to learn, I think he will need his heart and brain. Do you think you can remember the character now?'

Funnily enough, I think I can. I know what the character for scholar looks like and the character for heart is one of the first that I learned.

'Paulina!' Mrs Shen rushes over holding her fan, her face sweaty and pink from the exercise; her silver-grey curls are still in perfect shape, though. She ignores Xia, but inspects Mr Han with eager eyes. 'Will you introduce me to your friend?' she asks me.

'Han Weigang,' grumbles Mr Han, getting to his feet.

'How lovely to meet you,' gushes Mrs Shen. Before, I'd thought she only wanted to check who I was talking to, but now she is being so friendly I wonder what's going on.

The two of them start talking quickly, and it's a bit hard for me to follow their conversation. Mrs Shen smiles and laughs, but Weiting's grandad just grunts. Finally, he grabs Xia and walks away, not even saying goodbye.

'He's my friend's grandad,' I explain to Mrs Shen, who is tapping her fan in her hand. 'He's not very friendly; my friend did warn me.'

Mrs Shen stops her tapping. 'Has your friend told you more about his grandad?' she asks.

'Not much,' I reply. 'Only that it's his fault they had to move here from Taiwan. Weiting doesn't want to be here at all.'

'Well,' says Mrs Shen secretively, 'I actually know exactly who Mr Han is, since I have a special interest in calligraphy.'

I nod, because I've seen all the beautiful scrolls with Chinese characters on Mrs Shen's wall.

'Mr Han is a famous artist. He writes wonderful characters and his work is exhibited in museums all over the world. His artworks are very expensive.' She winks at me, and I'm not sure how to reply.

In the end, I say, 'Well, it doesn't matter how rich or famous he is – he certainly doesn't have the best manners.'

Chapter Thirteen

Mr Han's new characters are easier to learn, since they all have the character for heart within them. I have to look them up in a dictionary, as Mr Han hasn't translated them like Weiting does. I had no idea that there are so many words connected to heart – 'feeling', 'think', 'angry' and 'always', for example. To learn them I make up my own little stories about them just like Mr Han did in the park.

While I'm studying, I forget where I am, even down here under the stairs, surrounded by the cleaning stuff in semi-darkness.

'Hi,' says Weiting, suddenly crouching next to me.

I let my pen drop. 'You're back! I didn't see you in class this morning.'

'I wasn't.' He hesitates. 'I thought it would be better to start the day by meeting you here.'

I'm not sure if I should be flattered or worried, since Weiting looks really unwell. His face is pallid and much thinner than I remember.

'What's going on?' I ask. 'Your grandad said you had a fever.'

'He told me he met you – that's kind of why I'm here.' Weiting takes my book and flicks through it slowly. 'I see he couldn't stop himself showing off.' Frowning, he flicks through the pages featuring characters with a heart in them.

'Yeah, it doesn't really make much sense,' I lie. 'He didn't even write the translations.'

'He probably didn't talk about anything else but writing, right?' Weiting asks.

'He was mainly concentrating on Xia,' I say. 'And then he had to answer questions from our neighbour, Mrs Shen, who is extremely nosy.'

'The turtle, of course,' Weiting sighs. 'Why am I not surprised?'

He shuffles uncomfortably on the floor, as if his legs have grown a few inches since the last time we sat here. 'It's too silly,' he says finally. 'Just the stupid story of a grumpy old man who wants everything his own way. The biggest problem is that both my mum and dad work for him. So, he's not only the oldest in the family, he's also the one who controls all the money. My parents always do what he wants. Mum is actually a teacher, but she's given that up to sell his work.'

'He's an artist,' I say.

'I see – he's been boasting.'

'No, my neighbour told me. She recognized him at the park.'

'A lot of people back home know him, but they don't make a fuss. Everyone knows he likes to be left alone and only needs Xia for company.' He takes my book and scribbles in it. 'He prefers this: *gu*.'

'It means "alone".'

After the last few days at school with no one to play with, I can't understand how anyone would enjoy being alone. But at least Mr Han has Xia – maybe that makes all the difference.

'So what changed?' I ask, looking at the neat black drawing in its lonely box.

'One day in June, when we were back home in Taiwan, he sat down to breakfast and said, "Xia has made a wish." Mum and Dad looked at each other; I know they get concerned about him getting all strange. And I thought it was just a joke.'

Weiting lets his head droop almost on to his knees.

'Turns out that this wish involved us moving here, to Beijing – *Yeye's* old home. He explained to my parents that we all would benefit from a change of scenery. It would give him new ideas for his calligraphy, going back to his roots, and my parents could find new business contacts here. I wasn't really mentioned in the plans, apart from "young trees can easily be planted in new soil". That's all he said.' He looks up at me with dark eyes.

'But what did he mean by Xia making a wish?'

'He never said.' Weiting looks up hopefully. 'So, since you're the one he's been talking to, I was wondering if you could find out, because he also said that as soon as the wish is fulfilled, we can go home.'

My heart sinks. The last thing I want is for Weiting to go back home. He probably doesn't even realize he's the only friend I've got. But how can I say this to him, when he's so unhappy here and has asked me for a favour? What kind of friend would I be if I just put my own wishes before his?

Chapter Fourteen

I thought that it was a really long shot to expect me to extract the secret of Xia's wish from Mr Han – but I didn't have the heart to tell Weiting that. What's more, I owe him, not only for helping me with the books and teaching me Chinese, but also for standing by me at school. I'm constantly dreaming up plans for convincing everyone that Zoe was making up all those stories about me, but no one wants to be seen with me, let alone talk to me. It's almost as if they are afraid of what Zoe might do to them in return.

Focusing on the grandad mission means I find myself in the park more often than ever before. When Mum's busy, Mrs Shen walks me down there and keeps an eye on me from her fan-waving group.

I've met Mr Han and Xia three more times in the park. It's easy to bump into them; I just sit down wherever I like and eventually they appear. I've tried sitting in different places, like the wooden stools near the little shop that sells pancakes, or the pavilion on the small hill, with its beautiful view of the park. It usually takes Xia no longer than ten minutes to appear, and so far I've never managed to notice him approaching. He just seems to materialize sitting next to me. Within another minute or so, Mr Han always shows up. We never discuss why Xia seeks me out. Mr Han doesn't mention it, and I feel a bit guilty, as if the turtle is demonstrating to Mr Han that I'm his new favourite.

The afternoon breeze feels chilly, so I'm glad the stone I'm sitting on has been warmed by the sun. I'm looking around, hoping to catch Xia sneaking up on me, when I hear a rustling under the huge green leaves behind me. He's never found me so fast, I think. Or maybe it's the other way round; maybe I've found him today.

'Miss Sun!' Mr Han waves from the small wooden bridge that leads like a rainbow over a tiny stretch of water. I wave back and smile. 'How are your studies?' he calls. The old couple chatting to Mrs Shen stretch their necks to observe him. He makes his way to a small bench on the other side of the bridge and signals for me to come over.

I walk towards him, disregarding Xia, who will come in his own time.

'Now, "water",' says Mr Han as soon as I've reached him. He points at the little lake and the small streams feeding into it.

Silently, I give him my exercise book. Weiting has grudgingly accepted that his grandad now writes in it.

'*Shui*,' he says, and draws the character:

水

'You know that, right?'

I nod. It's a fairly easy character, consisting of just four strokes, and I like its strange symmetry.

'If water is used to form another character, it turns into *san dian shui* –'

氵

' – "three drops of water". Did you know that too?'

I do – it's easy to remember and very easy to recognize.

Mr Han begins drawing and naming characters that start with the three drops of water: '"River", "the sea" – they're all obvious, aren't they? But there are many more – *lei*, "tear", for example. "Three drops of water" and "an eye".'

泪

Of course, I can't tell Weiting, but I do enjoy these lessons and what I like most about them is the way Mr Han draws in my book, as if the pen was a paintbrush, making the characters look like tiny artworks – every stroke filled with detail.

'How did you become a calligraphy artist?' I ask when he's finished the character.

'Someone told me my writing was beautiful. A person who had a natural eye for talent and was not too envious to encourage me. I owe her more than I could ever pay back. That's how it started – the rest was pretty easy.' He fills what remains of the page with characters that all start with three drops of water.

'It still must've been hard work,' I say, imagining having to memorize thousands of characters and draw them all so beautifully.

He turns his head to me and focuses on my face, combing back his white hair with his hands. 'I once knew someone with the same curious grey eyes and the same accent as you. It was many years ago, but you very much remind me of her. It was in a different time,' Mr Han continues, 'and we had very little, but still everyone lived their lives as well as they could.'

He keeps the pen tightly in his fingers and seems to write characters in the air while he talks.

'See, when I was your age, you would see caravans of camels walking through the streets of Beijing, coming from the plains north of the city. Mules would pull carriages and people would travel on rickshaws. It was normal to eat out on the streets and you could get your hair cut by a barber on every busy road. People wouldn't have dogs as pets, but instead they walked around with birds with a string tied round their feet, perched on a peg that sat on their owner's shoulder.'

Mr Han's warm, clear voice helps me to see the city as it must have been, many years ago. 'I had so much freedom as a boy. We didn't live too far from here, though there was no public park back then. But the ruins of the temple existed, of course.'

He is talking about the temple of the Sun, right in the middle of the park. I didn't know it used to be in ruins, but there isn't time to ask now. Mr Han is still talking.

'This is where I first met her. This is where I made a very unusual friend. Or should I say two?'

Chapter Fifteen

Xia has found his way back to us. Today, he chooses to sit next to Mr Han's feet, the sun making his shell shine a dark, glossy olive. 'Xia!' says Mr Han. 'It was actually him who brought us together – can you believe it?'

I look at Xia's shell, trying to figure out a pattern in the random marks between the hexagons. 'Did you already have him when you were a little boy?' I ask.

He looks at me, wrinkling his nose. 'The question should be, "Did he already have me when I was a little boy?", don't you think?'

I do find it funny that Mr Han thinks he's the turtle's pet and not the other way round, but I just nod because I want him to continue with his story. Perhaps this will finally give me the clues I need to help Weiting.

'So, how did Xia find you?' I ask.

Mr Han sinks back into the bench and rubs his forehead as if his memories would become clearer that way. 'It was a Sunday morning in early spring. Rain had fallen overnight and the city smelled fresh and new. I had just picked up some garments that had been mended for my mother. The streets were empty and I enjoyed looking at the ancient houses, studying their curved slate roofs and wooden doors. I was in no hurry, so as I passed by the ruins of the temple I decided to have a little rest and eat a piece of *mantou* bread the seamstress had kindly given me.

'To my surprise, I was not the only one admiring the old stones that morning. A foreign lady greeted me in a friendly way when I approached. She was wearing a scarf over her head, but it didn't cover all of her light-brown hair. I had never spoken to a foreigner before and was immediately impressed with how she had mastered our language.'

For a moment he looks up at the sky, as if he thinks he could find the answer to a question up there, and sighs.

'What did you talk about?' I ask.

'This and that. The temple, of course, but also our everyday lives. She asked me about school and my parents, and told me about her husband. I can't remember all of that first conversation, but I won't forget the moment she suddenly looked up with her strange-coloured eyes and asked me with a smile, "Is that your turtle?"'

'So that's when Xia found you,' I cry.

'Indeed,' says Mr Han, 'it is. He just appeared that day, out of nowhere, as if he had been waiting for me.'

'Did you take him home with you?'

He laughs. It is the very first time I've heard his laughter – which sounds like a dog barking, only sadder, and it frightens me slightly. 'No, of course not. What do you think my parents would have said? "Just another mouth to feed," probably. If you want to know the truth, I was slightly scared of Xia when we first met. Just look at his ancient face and the gleaming eyes; I wouldn't have touched him for anything. And what if he had a real owner who might have thought I was stealing him?'

'What happened next? Who was this foreign lady and did you become friends with her, too?' I ask quickly, to encourage Mr Han to continue.

'After we had introduced ourselves properly, I asked her how she had learned our language so well. Just like you, she could roll her r's like a true Northerner.'

That makes me laugh, because it was the first thing I learned when we moved here. Lots of words end in a pirate style 'rrrr', a speciality of the Beijing dialect.

'She laughed too and said she hadn't learned it well at all. Apparently she had lived in Beijing for a few years already and was trying her best to fit in. I wondered if she had any children. She looked a bit younger than my mother, but for all the time that I knew her, I never dared to ask her age or any personal questions.

'And just like you,' says Mr Han, winking at me, 'she was not shy to talk, quite unlike me. She would ask question after question about life here in Beijing, and I was happy to answer them, since it made me feel a bit like a teacher. She would even call me teacher – *laoshi*. I never had a name for her other than Mrs Grace; she mentioned her last name once belonged to an ancient king. She told me it was her husband's name, and he worked here at the British Embassy. He spent a lot of time at work, so she was quite lonely, I think.'

In front of us a few leaves are moving gently on the pond, and I try to spot a bird or a frog, but with no luck.

'What about Xia?' I ask. 'Was he living near the temple at that time?'

'I think so,' Mr Han says slowly. 'It became my habit to meet Mrs Grace at the temple, two or three afternoons a week and always on a Saturday morning. My parents encouraged me to go. They thought Mrs Grace could teach me some English, and I tried my hardest. However, even today I still struggle with your language.' He pauses and smiles. 'After a while she asked me to teach her some Chinese characters. She was the first person who mentioned that I had a talent for writing. My characters were like classical paintings, she said. And whenever we met, Xia would join us. It was as if he had become a part of our meeting, just like the temple, and the Chinese characters we would write on paper, or in the sand or even in the air.'

He starts to draw in the air again and it looks very much like the movements Mrs Shen and her friends make with their fans – completely smooth, with no hesitation at all.

After looking at the water for a while, I dare to ask, 'Do you know what—' but Mr Han doesn't let me finish my sentence.

'No,' he says, in a weak voice. 'I have no idea what happened to her and neither has Xia. She simply stopped coming to the park. After a week or so, I went to the Embassy to ask for her, but the gates were closed, and no one would answer my calls. I returned to the temple every day, but there was only Xia waiting for me. And when, only a short while later, my parents told me we were moving to Taiwan, I secretly decided to take Xia with me. I never heard a word from Mrs Grace again.'

And as soon as he has spoken these words, I feel like I understand why the turtle made his wish.

Chapter Sixteen

Weiting is in the worst mood today, almost ripping my exercise book in half while he flicks through its pages, making tiny crosses next to the characters I haven't written correctly. Even the crosses look angry.

'Are you writing any new characters in?' I ask, re-arranging a few of the new plastic buckets the cleaners have left under the stairs so they don't take up so much space. For once, I don't mind Weiting being moody, as I've actually had a fairly good week. A new boy and girl have arrived in our class and Mrs Wen has seated them on either side of me. She asked me to show them around the school and both of them seem really nice. Even better, neither of them seem to have attracted Zoe's attention, but I'm still wary of crossing paths with her.

'Why would I? *Yeye* has given you plenty to study, I can see.'

'I still like it better when you give me homework,' I explain. 'Your grandad won't even write the translation and he doesn't bother with the stroke order.'

'Believe me – he doesn't bother with anything,' Weiting grumbles. 'All he cares about is himself. Mum and Dad are worrying we'll never get back home.'

With a sudden kick, he destroys my new arrangement

of buckets, which roll over the floor and out of our hiding place.

'Why are you so angry?' I ask when the noise has died down. 'Are you homesick, like your parents?'

'He's just so selfish,' Weiting says. 'How can the turtle be more important than us? My friend emailed me yesterday from Taiwan. I'm in a basketball team back home and we've been doing pretty well. At least, we were while I was still playing for them. They've lost four times in a row now, and all they ask is when I'll be back. *Yeye* heard me complaining to Mum and Dad about it and you know what he said?'

I shrug my shoulders.

'He said, "How can the boy be upset about a sports team? He has the opportunity to live in one of the most historic cities in the world, but instead of exploring it, he complains about a silly game where you have to shoot a ball through a hoop. You've truly spoilt him!"'

I feel a momentary burst of anger at Mr Han, but then I remember his strange, sad laughter. I did tell Weiting about the mysterious woman his grandad knew and about the way he first met Xia. It didn't impress him very much.

Next to Weiting is a pile of library books that we still haven't sorted. He takes one of them and scans through the blurb. 'Don't you ever want to go back home to England?' he asks, without looking at me.

'Sure,' I say, 'one day, but ... ' I only finish the sentence in my head.

'But?' says Weiting, observing my face as if trying to read the answer to his question there.

'I'm not sure I'll still fit in.' It comes out easier than I expected, especially for a thought that I've had for weeks now and that's been growing stronger every day.

Weiting sighs. 'I never thought that this business with Zoe would get to you so much. I've never met a person who cared less about what other people think of her or how to fit in. You even wear non-matching socks! That's why your Chinese is so good.'

'Because of my different-coloured socks?' I ask.

'No,' he laughs, 'because you don't mind making mistakes. You just talk and learn, and if things go wrong, you get on with it. That's why you're so fluent.'

Shaking his head, he points at my socks, and I start laughing. Maybe he has a point.

Chapter Seventeen

'Paulina, you really need new shoes,' cries Mum, inspecting my worn-out trainers. 'There's no way you can walk for a whole day with these in Longqing Gorge.'

'Longqing Gorge?' I say excitedly. 'I had no idea that was where we were going!'

The gorge is one of the most beautiful places I know and we haven't been there since spring. I can't wait to get out of the city and go to a place that looks like an ancient Chinese landscape painting.

'We'll set off next Saturday morning; you can't imagine how much I need a break.' I absolutely can. Mum has dark shadows under her eyes, evidence she has been working too much and sleeping too little. 'It'll be getting colder soon. This might be our last chance to go before the temperature drops and it's no fun any more.'

'Are we staying at the same guest house?' I remember the neat little building in the middle of the forest, by an impressive waterfall.

'Yes, we are, but this time we will have to book three rooms, so all six of us have a place to stay.'

I look at Mum without understanding, although a dark thought creeps into my head.

'Come on,' she says cheerfully. 'I've told you before, haven't I? We really wanted to spend time with Susan, Tim and Zoe. So, they've agreed to join us on the trip. It'll be fun.'

Whatever she says next, I can't hear her. I feel a strong sensation in my stomach, and it's creeping up all the way to my mouth. 'Mum,' I interrupt her, 'can I please go to the park?' I don't wait for her answer, slipping my feet into the worn-out trainers as quickly as I can and running out of the front door.

Mum follows me silently down Guanghua Road. Thin, cold drops of rain start to fall, but I hardly notice. The park is almost deserted, because the autumn wind is blowing fiercely today. I very much doubt that Mr Han and Xia will be here either, but just in case, I cool my face with my ice-cold hands and practise a smile. But no matter how much I try to pretend, it's not working. How could Mum do that? A day and a night in the mountains with Zoe, where our parents will make us share a room.

The rain is getting stronger and the wind colder. Even the big tree doesn't offer much shelter.

'Paulina,' says Mum gently, putting her hand on my shoulder. She opens an umbrella. 'Let's just go back home.'

'I just want to have a look in there,' I say, pointing to a visitor information hut. I run towards it before Mum objects.

I dash through the puddles that seem to have appeared out of nowhere, splashing my trousers with mud. Finally, I reach the hut and barge the door open. It's almost empty, apart from an older couple who are sitting on a bench under a row of old photographs, with steaming cups in their hands.

'What a storm!' says the man in a friendly voice, very slowly, not sure if I can understand him.

'It is,' I say, pointing at drops falling from my clothes to the ground. '*Linshi le* – I'm soaked.'

'I like your accent,' says the lady, making room for me to sit down.

I move closer but instead of sitting down I begin to study the black and white photographs on the wall.

'All pictures of the Sun temple,' says the man, sipping from his cup. 'You know how long ago it was built? Almost five hundred years ago – but then it all got destroyed.'

'Right,' I say. I had asked Mrs Shen about the history of the temple earlier. 'But they rebuilt it before they opened the park, didn't they?'

'You know a lot,' says the lady, smiling at me.

Most of the photographs are of the construction site, of workers pulling up huge stones and planting trees. I can't read any of the captions, though I am able to recognize a few characters. There's a whole row of black and white photographs featuring serious, besuited men holding what look like plans or certificates up to the camera. But then I notice something else. Among the Chinese men stands a foreign couple, both dressed in white. The man has an impressive moustache and the woman wears a beautiful wide-brimmed hat.

Among the Chinese characters in the caption for this picture is a single English word: 'Solomon'.

'Excuse me,' I ask the couple, 'could you read this to me? I don't recognize all the characters.' I point to the bottom of the picture.

'Of course,' says the lady. 'It states here that "the official beginning of the temple's reconstruction started with a celebration, attended by ... "' she starts reading out a list of a few Chinese names, '" ... and by Mr and Mrs Solomon from the British Embassy."'

Behind me the door of the hut opens. Mum reaches out her hand to touch my shoulder, but I'm too excited to say a word. I just stare at the old photograph in front of me, trying to organize my thoughts.

And then, it's easy to understand. I look at the face of the woman in the picture, half shaded by her wide-brimmed hat, but even so, her expression of clever curiosity is clear.

And now I know her name, I hear Mr Han's voice in my head – 'an ancient king': a wise king like King Solomon. It's her in the picture – it's Mrs Grace.

Chapter Eighteen

I haven't told Weiting about my discovery, nor have I talked to Mr Han about it.

First, I need to find out more about Mrs Grace Solomon. This proves to be much harder than I thought. The Internet doesn't come up with anything. Of course there are hundreds of Grace Solomons around the world, but they all look young. The one I'm looking for must be almost a hundred years old by now.

It's Mrs Lundman who gives me the right idea, when she finds me on the library computer one day and I explain that I am looking for someone who lived in China about seventy years ago.

'Haven't I told you that you can find the answers to all your questions in a book? Have you even tried that yet?'

Again, the question is how to get my hands on the right book. The answer is so obvious that I wonder how I didn't think of it right away. If you need to find out about the past, who better to ask than someone who writes about it for a living?

'Mum,' I say after school, 'how do you find out about someone who lived in Beijing many years ago?'

She takes off her glasses and rests her chin on her hand. 'What do you mean by "many years"? Are you looking for a particular historical figure or is this a general question?'

I sometimes forget that Mum is obsessed with people being precise. Dad says this is what makes her a good historian.

'You remember Mr Han? Weiting's grandad? When he was young and lived in Beijing, he knew a lady whose husband worked at the British Embassy,' I begin. 'I think I've discovered her in one of the photographs in the information hut in the park – her and her husband. The picture was taken at about the time they renovated the temple.'

'That was at the beginning of the 1950s,' Mum says instantly, and it doesn't surprise me that she knows this. Somehow she manages to keep the facts from all the books she reads in her head.

'Can you help me to find out what happened to Mr Han's friend?' I ask. 'Her name is Grace Solomon.'

* * *

Forty-five minutes later, we're in the National Library. Mum leads the way, and I have a feeling she knows exactly where we're going. I just follow her, gazing up at the massive glass ceiling and marvelling at the walls lined with shelves, holding what looks like millions of books.

'This is it,' she says finally, when we arrive at a rather

unspectacular-looking table in a corner. 'Wait here – I'll be back in a moment.'

Soon she comes back with three big volumes bound in blue, with battered brown pages.

'These are records of all the British diplomats in Beijing up to the 1960s. Let's see if we can find the Solomons.'

* * *

'Here!' I say, as their names suddenly jump out of the page. '"Richard Solomon, wife Grace, son Henry."'

Mum studies the page carefully. 'It seems that Richard was the assistant to the British Ambassador at the time. He came here in 1947 and left in 1950. Look here. Their son Henry was born in 1951, after they returned home to Liverpool.'

I'm so excited that I've found Grace, I forget we're in a library and speak far too loudly. 'And that's where we'll find her! I'm sure she still lives in Liverpool.'

Mum touches my arm gently. 'Paulina,' she says, 'look at those dates. There's a fair chance that Grace might not be alive any more.'

I don't really listen, because too much is going on in my head. If I can find Grace, it will make Mr Han so happy. After all that he has told me, discovering what happened to his old friend must be the reason he's here, even though he tells everyone it's Xia's wish. I can't wait to tell Weiting about it.

Chapter Nineteen

The same evening, a more focused search with Dad brought a result. The words 'Solomon', 'Grace', 'Henry', 'Liverpool' and 'China' led us to a famous antique shop in England. OK, so Grace wasn't mentioned on the shop's website at all, but who else could the owner Henry Solomon be, other than her son?

Dad helped me to write an email to the shop, explaining that I was doing research on Grace and Richard, and how I came to know about them through meeting Mr Han and Xia.

For four days I've been waiting for a reply, but Dad says so far there's no email from Henry Solomon. I could just call the number on the website, but I know Mum and Dad don't want me to hassle Henry, especially after they've told me to be patient.

Today is not the day for it anyway. It's the most miserable Saturday ever. Dad and Mum have packed their bags and Dad is about to finish a call before we head off to Longqing Gorge, for the dreaded outing with Zoe and her family.

All week I've been trying to persuade Mum to cancel the trip, and I even started to tell her about Zoe's behaviour at school, but she refused to listen. She's so eager to see her own friends, it's almost as if she can't bear to believe that Zoe isn't one of mine.

* * *

I'm standing in front of my wardrobe and can't decide whether I should wear my warm black jacket with the silken embroidered dragon wriggling across its back, or my boring grey hoody. Of course, Zoe will giggle about the jacket, but she'll find some way to make fun of me, no matter what I wear. I might as well wear the jacket and be nice and cosy.

Maybe we'll eat at the hot pot restaurant again, and I can smuggle some of the bitter Chinese broccoli leaves into her bowl. The thought makes me smile and I don't hear the door to my room opening. Mum looks flustered. 'You have a visitor, but remember, we need to leave in five minutes.' Behind her stands Weiting.

I'm so surprised that I let my jacket drop to the floor. Weiting watches Mum leave, and when he turns around I see that there are tiny beads of sweat on his forehead and his hair is messier than usual.

'You need to help me,' he says, putting a big canvas bag carefully on my bed.

'What's wrong?' I ask, sitting next to his bag and thoughtlessly throwing a few clothes into my backpack.

87

'Something is seriously wrong with *Yeye*. He's made up his mind. He told us a few nights ago that he wants to sell our house back home and that we should move to Beijing for good. Mum and Dad were as shocked as I was, but he said we would have to do it for him, and that always persuades them. But even worse, now he's gone completely quiet; he doesn't even seem to care about Xia any more. If it wasn't for me, he would have left Xia behind in the park twice this week. That gave me an idea – what if Xia goes missing? Maybe he will start caring again, and maybe he will finally talk to my parents about what is going on.'

Weiting paces up and down my room. I try to stop him by standing in front of him.

'You have to help me. *Yeye* would trust Xia with you more than anyone. Just take good care of him for one or two days.' Weiting points a finger to the bag on my bed.

When I look at it, the bag seems to move, which makes me jump.

Weiting pulls the bag open. I can't believe my eyes – there, in front of me, sits a turtle. Weiting has kidnapped Xia!

Chapter Twenty

I wonder how Weiting assumes that I can take care of Xia while I'm on a trip.

'Paulina, we need to go,' Mum shouts from the hall.

Weiting is looking at me with eyes almost as intense as Xia's. 'You have to take care of Xia. I am sure *Yeye* will come to his senses once he starts missing him. I don't want *Yeye* to be unhappy, but maybe he'll realize that letting us all go home again is the right thing to do for our family.'

Then he sees my backpack. He takes Xia and puts him carefully inside. 'Just take him with you for the weekend,' he says. '*Yeye* once said that Xia especially enjoys the fresh mountain air.'

There are so many reasons why I disagree with Weiting that I cannot say a single word. The words have all become an insoluble lump that blocks my speech.

The door opens, but before Mum can speak, Weiting backs out, calling, 'I need to go too. Thanks for explaining the homework, Paulina. Have a good trip, Mrs Taylor.'

Mum looks at me suspiciously, but Dad is calling her to help him with the bags. I stand paralysed while she grabs my backpack with Xia in it.

'Mum, I haven't finished packing,' I stumble. But she just walks out, saying, 'This backpack feels heavy enough for me. How much stuff do you need for one night?'

For a moment I don't know what to do. How can Weiting even think that this will solve his problems? If we'd had a few more minutes, I could've told him about Grace Solomon and convinced him to take Xia back. I race to the door, trying to see if Weiting is still around, but he has left.

The last thing I see through the elevator's closing door is Dad amongst our bags, holding my backpack in his hands.

* * *

I'm so glad that Dad has put my backpack on the seat next to me. I immediately check on Xia, and with my hands inside the backpack, I settle him on one of my jumpers, hoping it will make a nice blanket for him to sit on.

During the drive, I sometimes whisper to him gently, bearing in mind that he doesn't like to be touched. But just having him here gives me a calm and peaceful feeling, and strangely, I feel quite glad to have a quiet companion around.

* * *

The air is much cooler when we get out of the car, but I hardly feel it as I take in the magical landscape around us. The trees are shimmering in gold and red on the cliffs that line the riverbanks left and right. But my excitement vanishes as soon as I see that the others have arrived. Mum and Susan wave at each other, and I spot Zoe immediately. She's trailing behind her parents, her hair arranged in a perfectly neat bun.

'I love this,' says Tim. 'What a wonderful place, and it seems we've come just at the right time. Zoe, look at the colour of those trees.'

Without even glancing up, Zoe mumbles a 'Yes, great,' and at this moment, I'm sure that I'm not the only one dreading this trip. But I have bigger worries than Zoe right now, because all I can think about is Xia in my bag. In the car, I was able to check on him constantly. Now, I have to sit next to Zoe on a boat trip. We're travelling slowly down the river, but Zoe is not looking up at the cliffs that fall sharply into the water or at the amazingly blue river. She is staring down at the floor, where I keep my backpack safe between my feet.

I'm relieved when we can get off the boat and start our hike to the gorge. Zoe lets herself fall behind and we have to wait for her to catch up. From time to time, Mum whispers, 'Can you be a bit friendlier?' But honestly, I quite enjoy the silence between Zoe and me. There really isn't much to say.

* * *

In the evening, we're all exhausted from walking for hours in the fresh mountain air and, more than anything else, I'm starving. The restaurant here is famous and Dad tells everyone how lucky we are to get a table. We're about to eat hot pot, which is a bit like fondue. It's a boiling broth with different meats and vegetables served in a big pot in the middle of the table. When I look at the menu, I'm pleased that I can recognize the two characters that make the name 'hot pot' – *huoguo* – which are 'fire' and 'pot':

火锅

'Zoe, what vegetables or meat would you like?' Mum asks, but Zoe only shrugs.

While Zoe is struggling with her chopsticks, I fill the boiling pot with shrimp, fish and my favourite mushrooms. The steam rises into my nose and I can't wait for the food to be ready.

'Can you go and ask for more water?' Dad says, and I jump up quickly to find the waitress.

A minute later, I'm back with a jug of warm water to fill up our pot. The grown-ups are laughing, but it is impossible to follow the conversation over the hubbub of the busy restaurant.

As I sit down, I glance at Zoe, who is staring at the ground again. Only this time, it's not out of boredom or to avoid me. This time she is concentrating on my open backpack, where Xia is clearly visible now, stretching out his neck, and winking at both of us.

Chapter Twenty-One

'Please don't!' I mouth, terrified that Zoe will scream, or point out Xia to our parents, or do anything else that would betray his presence.

But she just looks at Xia with such a surprised expression that all I can do is carefully close the backpack without looking at her. She doesn't say a word at first, but it feels like she is almost smiling when, finally, she asks in a very soft voice, 'Can you fish some of the noodles out for me, Paulina? I really can't handle these chopsticks.'

* * *

We're in our room about two hours later. Dinner turned out to be completely different from what I expected. It was as if Zoe changed into a different person. At first, she was quiet, chewing on the long white rice noodles, but then she became more interested in the conversation and started to answer Mum's questions about her life back in England. For the first time, Zoe's brother was mentioned: he seemed to be a kind of science genius and was away at boarding school doing his GCSEs. When I asked Zoe if she missed him, Zoe just grinned and said, 'Not one bit! He is such a nerd,' but I could hear in her voice that she liked him a lot. At one point, Zoe started to taste tiny scraps of food from the hot pot and made everyone laugh when she made a half curious, half disgusted face at the texture.

'Finally,' she says now, falling on to the bed by the window. The night is pitch black and all sounds are muffled by the rushing of the big waterfall in the distance. 'I'm kind of glad that we're sharing a room – now you can tell me all about the tortoise. I guess your parents have no idea you brought a pet on the trip.'

'He is an American box turtle,' I say sternly and look at Zoe suspiciously. She seems almost too innocent in her cuddly white onesie, hugging her knees tightly to her body. What is she planning?

'Come on,' Zoe says. 'If I'd wanted to get you into trouble, don't you think I would have done it in the restaurant? Honestly, I won't tell on you. I've done stupid things before too.'

'It's not exactly easy to trust you, after what you've been saying about me at school,' I start, putting the backpack carefully on the bed. 'I don't understand why you've been telling all those lies about me.'

'They weren't exactly lies,' Zoe says, shifting backwards and forwards on the bed. At least she has the decency to look uncomfortable. 'I just thought I was telling a few funny stories. You did say all that stuff about the dolls and food when I was over at your place. I just turned it around a bit. And then, I guess I liked that everyone was listening to me. Especially since I didn't know anyone at first ... '

But suddenly I can't hear a word of what Zoe is saying. All I can do is stare in panic at my backpack. I'm so sure that I closed it in the restaurant, before we walked to the guest house. Why is the zip open, and where is Xia? I dig deeper among my clothes and turn the backpack inside out. I find absolutely nothing – Xia has gone.

Zoe is almost as eager to find the turtle as I am. Anxiously, she begins to search the room. We look under the bed, in the cupboard, and in the tiny bathroom. There's no trace of Xia. I collapse on the bed, thinking about what Mr Han will say if I can't return his beloved friend.

'Come on,' I hear Zoe say, and feel a hand on my shoulder. 'We'll go back to the restaurant and look for him.'

'Why are you suddenly acting like you care?' I snap at Zoe. As if losing Xia isn't bad enough, the last thing I need is Zoe storing up information about this disaster to share with her cronies back at school. I'm so angry with Weiting for putting me in this position I could burst into tears.

'I know I've been pretty awful to you, but I'm not heartless, Paulina,' says Zoe, sitting down next to me. 'I love animals. Back in England I had two rabbits and a cat, and when we moved here we had to find new homes for them. I really miss them, so I'd hate to think of anyone else losing their pet. I know how much being separated from them hurts.'

Maybe Mum is right; maybe there is more going on with Zoe than I realized. But that's a thought that will have to wait until we've found Xia.

Chapter Twenty-Two

It's past midnight when we leave the guest house entrance and walk the narrow, stony path to the restaurant in the grounds. The night air is cool and dry, but I can feel the sweat on my neck as we walk as quickly as we can.

'I'm sure the restaurant will be closed by now,' I say anxiously to Zoe. 'We were among the last guests to leave.'

Zoe gently rubs my elbow and I can't help but feel comforted. At least I'm not alone looking for Xia, and even if it's Zoe with me, I need all the help I can get to find him.

'Will you tell me now why you're carrying this turtle around?' asks Zoe, when we have almost reached the restaurant.

'First of all, he's not my turtle,' I start. I don't know how to tell Zoe about Xia. After all, the story is complicated and I don't want to give away too much about Weiting: that would feel like a betrayal.

'A friend asked me to take care of him over the weekend. The turtle's name is Xia. I think he must be almost a hundred years old.'

'OK,' says Zoe, 'but why did you have to drag him

along to the mountains? Couldn't your friend find someone else to look after him?'

I hesitate. 'Please don't make fun of me again, but Xia seems to like me. He usually comes with my friend to the park and roams around quite freely. Somehow, he always seems to find me. That's probably why my friend thought I would be the right person to look after him.'

When we're finally standing in front of the restaurant, my heart sinks. Not a single light shines through the narrow windows and the door is locked. Zoe rings the bell next to the entrance, but there's no reply.

I feel my legs shaking. I sit down on the ground, my back against a huge tree. The moon has come out from behind the clouds and is suddenly shining so brightly that the trees and plants around us are flooded with a beautiful white light.

And then I feel Zoe's arm around my shoulder. 'Don't worry,' she says. 'We'll find the turtle. Although it sounds as though it's the turtle who usually finds you.'

We sit and wait and huddle closer together as the cold rises from the ground.

'I'm sorry,' Zoe says after a long silence. 'I know that what I did at school was wrong. It's just that I was so angry about being here, especially since it was all my fault.'

'What do you mean?' I ask.

'I failed the entrance exam to my brother's school back home. It's really hard to get a place there, but my parents expected me to. I heard Mum talking to Dad one night when they thought I wasn't listening. She said that now he could take the job offer in Beijing, where I would definitely get into a good school. So in a way it's really down to me that Mum and Dad relocated here. But I didn't want to come. And then when we got here and met you, Mum just wouldn't stop talking about you and how well you'd adjusted to Beijing life. I felt as though I couldn't stand you, even though we'd only just met.'

I close my eyes and exhale. It feels as if I have been holding my breath since the beginning of term. I'm so relieved that Zoe has finally apologized to me. What if this means that we could actually become friends?

Before I can say anything, something rustles near our feet. Zoe squeals, but I stay calm, because I have a strange, wonderful feeling. And I'm right: there in front of us, glimmering in the moonlight, sits Xia.

I scoop him up with both hands, like I've seen Mr Han do, and press him gently to my chest. He has retracted into his shell, but I can feel his tiny heart bumping slowly against my own. I've never been so happy to see him.

* * *

We wake early the next morning, too excited about our midnight adventure to lie in. I'm so relieved to have found Xia that I can't stop talking about him to Zoe. I find myself telling her the whole story of everything that's been happening to me the past few weeks.

At last, Dad comes in to see if we're awake. If he's surprised to see Zoe sitting cheerfully on my bed, he doesn't show it.

'I thought I should come and show you this, Paulina. This email came for you last night. I have a feeling you'll be very pleased to read it.'

He leaves his phone and smiles at Zoe before he closes the door.

I fall back on the bed next to Zoe and start reading the email that Henry Solomon has sent me. Zoe reads with me and when we're done, she smiles at me broadly.

When Zoe and I run excitedly into the breakfast room together, Mum and Susan shoot each other secret, satisfied looks.

'So, girls,' Mum says happily, 'do you want to hang around here for a bit, or do another walk today, or head straight back to the city?'

When we both shout, 'Go back!' Mum looks disappointed, but only for a moment, because I add quickly, 'Can Zoe come to ours tomorrow so I can show her the park?' Mum, Dad, Tim and Susan all agree that this is an excellent idea. One way or another, the trip has been a success after all.

Chapter Twenty-Three

My stomach feels a bit weird, but as the car pulls into Guanghua Road, I carefully take Xia out of my backpack. 'Mum, Dad, there is something I want to tell you.'

Mum gives a loud shriek when she sees Xia on the back seat and Dad immediately pulls over and stops the car.

'Paulina, why is there a tortoise sitting next to you?' he asks, sounding more surprised than angry. After hearing my explanation, Dad turns the car around and we head straight to Weiting's apartment.

* * *

My hands are shaking when I press the doorbell. What if nobody is at home? But a few seconds later, the door is opened by a friendly-looking woman.

'I'm Paulina,' I start, but the lady quickly interrupts.

'Of course you are,' she cries. 'I've heard so much about you. I'm Weiting's mum. And these are your parents, I guess?'

Mum and Dad shake hands with Weiting's mum and she beckons us inside.

'My dad had a feeling we might have visitors today,' Weiting's mum says, 'which is why I've prepared some snacks. Take a seat and I'll get the rest of the family.'

The room is big and cosy, all the walls covered in calligraphic scrolls featuring bold characters so artistically drawn that they are almost impossible to recognize. Right next to the big round table hangs a scroll with just one character – a scholar and a heart. I remember Mr Han telling me that it meant 'ambition'.

Soon, the door opens and in comes Mr Han with a younger man – presumably Weiting's dad. The last person to enter is Weiting. I feel far too anxious to look him in the eye, but he seems very relaxed, with his hands in the pockets of his jeans and his hair falling slightly over his eyes.

'See, Grandson,' says Mr Han, 'I told you she'd be here today, and she even brought her family.'

Chapter Twenty-Four

The tea smells strong and smoky, but I'm too nervous to drink it or eat one of the delicious cakes that Weiting's mum is offering us.

Weiting was right. I do talk a lot when I'm nervous, and the words start tumbling out of my mouth. 'I've looked after Xia,' I say, watching Weiting out of the corner of my eye, but I can't see the expression on his face. 'I really hope you weren't too worried,' I continue, putting Xia gently on the stone floor.

'Oh, Miss Sun,' says Mr Han, 'I never worry about Xia. He's always where he wants to be. I thought you would have known that by now.'

My face turns hot. 'Of course. I came to return him, but there's also something very important I want to show you.' I pull out Dad's phone and switch it on; it's still on the email that I've read a million times since last night.

Now Mr Han looks surprised. He might have known I would return Xia to him, but he clearly has no idea what I'm talking about.

'It's an email from Mrs Grace's son, Henry. He lives in Liverpool in England, and it wasn't easy to find him. But please, just listen and you'll understand.'

I see Weiting whispering to his mum, who shakes her head in disbelief.

I translate the email for them. "'Dear Paulina,'" I start, "'how wonderful that you got in touch with me. I was so surprised and delighted to receive your email. Let me answer your biggest question right at the beginning. You've found the right Henry Solomon. My mother Grace and my father Richard spent five years in China, leaving the country before I was born. I have travelled to Beijing many times since, and I even know the park you mentioned in your email. My mother told me all about it.'"

Weiting's dad tries to speak to Mr Han, but Mr Han just raises a hand to ask for silence.

"'Of course I know who your dear friend Mr Han is, and I'm so touched that you contacted me on his behalf. In fact, I should have written to Mr Han many years ago, because my mother never did.

"'That doesn't mean she didn't care. You should know that she often mentioned the shy boy with this fantastic talent who taught her so much about China, and she also talked about his unusual friendship with a turtle.'"

When I look up, I can see a tear rolling down Mr Han's cheek, so I try my best to translate quickly.

"'I remember the day, many years ago, when my mother showed me an article about a calligraphy artist in Taiwan.

She had recognized Mr Han and was so excited that he had fulfilled his dreams. But instead of contacting him, she made me buy some of his work, which we sold in our shop, here in Liverpool. Can you imagine?

"'I asked her to get in touch, but she only said, 'Why would he want to hear from an old lady from his childhood?' But I know how much she regretted that she never had the opportunity to say goodbye to Mr Han. My parents left China almost overnight when my father was called back to England for work. They had intended to return, but then I came along and my parents decided to raise their family in England.

"'My mother passed away twelve years ago, having lived a full life with her four children and seven grandchildren, and we will always remember her for her fantastic storytelling and the encouragement she gave to others.

"'Please give Mr Han my very best wishes and tell him I would love to meet him in person one day.'"

I finish reading, and the only sound is Xia shuffling on the floor.

'Thank you, Miss Sun,' Mr Han says eventually. 'Please write back to Mr Henry Solomon to tell him that he can visit me any time he likes, but he will need to come to Taiwan because we will soon be returning home.'

* * *

Mr Han asks Mum and Dad if I may join him and Xia on a little walk, and they both agree. Everyone says goodbye, and Weiting's mum, beaming broadly, makes us promise to come back soon. I walk down the busy road with Mr Han. He holds Xia on his arm and looks down at the turtle thoughtfully.

'I have to thank you, Miss Sun; you have done a lot for me and I will never forget it. How did you find out about Xia's wish?'

'I only guessed,' I reply. 'After all that you've told me about Mrs Grace, I thought that must surely be why you came back to Beijing. To find out what had happened to her.'

Mr Han looks at me. 'I was very upset that I couldn't say goodbye to my friend, and it bothered me all those years. Now, I understand. Mrs Grace had even told me that although she loved China, one day she would return to England to raise her children. I'm glad that she lived her life just as she had imagined it.

'Xia has been a constant reminder of Mrs Grace. I think without her I might have given up on calligraphy before it became my profession. In a way I think Mrs Grace is still encouraging me through him. When I look at Xia, I hear her voice saying, "Keep studying, you have a talent." Please, Miss Sun, take a look at this.'

Mr Han puts Xia down on a bench and points to some markings on the lower left side of his shell.

'Can you see that?'

I squint. 'It almost looks like the character *zhao*,' I say.

找

'Right!' exclaims Mr Han. 'How wonderful that your reading has improved so much. It does indeed look like the character *zhao*, which means "to search". I only saw the marks a few months ago. Who knows, maybe they were there all the time, but in my head, I thought it was a message. I thought it meant I was supposed to come back here and look for her. But instead of finding Grace, I've found you. Or, to be precise – Xia found you.'

I stare at the markings that look so faint and pale.

'Are you sad that she's dead?' I ask.

'I thought I would be, but I'm relieved that she lived a long and happy life. She put her family first, which is what I should do. I have not been a very good grandfather. I realized that, when Xia was gone. It didn't take me long to figure out that Weiting was responsible for Xia's disappearance. It seems he wanted to wake me up – and it worked! I gave more attention to the wishes of Xia than to the wishes of my grandson. But I promise I will do better, once we're back home. Maybe I'll even watch one of those basketball games.'

I'm not sure how to reply, so I simply say, 'I will miss you, when you're gone,' which is the truth.

Chapter Twenty-Five

Two months later

'How do you know all these characters?' Alin asks me, tracing my writing in the sand.

'I've been studying secretly,' I reply, laughing.

'That's amazing,' Alin says. 'One day, you'll probably be teaching me.'

It's the last morning before the Christmas break, and we're standing under the sycamore trees in the playground, shivering. Zoe comes running over wearing my black dragon jacket that she borrowed from me, and the wind has made her face go completely red.

'Can I please keep your jacket for the holidays?' she asks and I nod. She'll need it for her visit to England, but Mum, Dad and I are flying to Taiwan, where it's nice and warm, to visit Weiting and his family.

'Are you taking Xia with you on holiday?' she asks, rubbing her hands to warm them.

'It's too complicated,' I say, 'so Mrs Shen is taking care of him. Not that she likes Xia very much: she says he reminds her of a dinosaur. But how could we take Xia on a plane? I don't think he wants to do any more travelling.'

'Don't you think Mr Han would be happy to see him?' Zoe asks.

'I guess, but he said he can wait until Chinese New Year, which is when he comes over anyway. It will be so exciting, because that's when he's meeting Henry Solomon for the first time!'

Zoe giggles. 'It always makes me laugh when I think about your parents seeing Xia in the back of the car. I love it when you tell that story. Although I still can't believe Mr Han decided to leave Xia with you when they went home.'

I laugh. 'You should have seen Mum and Dad's faces when he said, "This turtle has found your daughter; it is his wish to stay with her."'

We laugh and laugh until tears run down our faces. I'm so glad that Zoe and I are friends now. I've never met anyone who can make me laugh as much as she does. Finally, Zoe calms down and says very seriously: 'Well, I must say, this turtle made a good choice.'